WHEN DISASTER STRIKES

EXTREME FIRES AND FLOODS

by John Farndon

HUNGRY TOMATO

CONTENTS

WILDFIRES

Wildfires are uncontrolled fires that sweep across field and forest. They can burn for days or weeks, wiping out all life over vast areas, and threatening human settlements close by. They may be ignited by the glow from a discarded cigarette or a stray ember from a barbecue, which turns an entire forest into a raging inferno, consuming everything in its path.

FLOODS

A flood happens when a lot of water suddenly submerges normally dry land. It can rise and recede quickly in a 'flash' flood after an intense storm, or build up slowly and last for months. Severe floods can be devastating, swamping vast regions and destroying people's homes and livelihoods, often claiming many lives.

HOW DOES A WILDFIRE HAPPEN?

Wildfires start when some kind of spark ignites dry vegetation. They occur wherever there is enough moisture to let trees and bushes grow, but where there are long warm, dry summers. As the heat of summer dries them out, the trees and bushes turn into a giant pile of firewood and kindling – just waiting for that dangerous spark to set them alight.

UNBELIEVABLE!

In 2012, nearly 10 million acres of forest burned in the USA – an area bigger than New Jersey, Connecticut and Delaware combined. On average, twice as large an area of forest burns in the USA now as it did 40 years ago.

CROWN OF FIRE

Wildfires can burn in different ways. Ground fires burn slowly in the soil, consuming the organic material there. Surface fires spread rapidly along the ground burning fallen leaves and branches. Crown fires are the most dramatic of all, burning ferociously with huge flames that spread from treetop to treetop, catching all alight.

FIERY TRIANGLE

To burn, a fire needs three things, sometimes called the fire triangle: fuel, oxygen and heat. The fuel is provided by vegetation. Oxygen comes from the air — when fuel burns, it reacts with the oxygen. Heat comes from the spark that starts the fire, or from the fire itself, once it is going. The fire will only stop when deprived of one of these three.

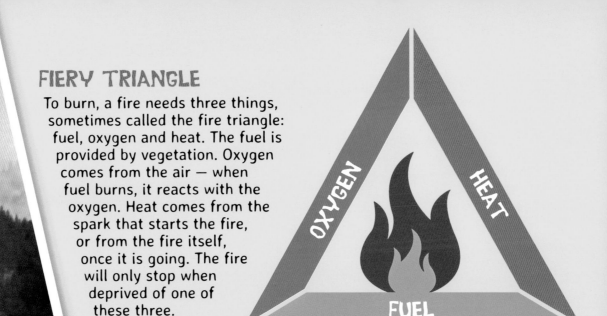

FIRE WHIRLS

Wildfires, especially big crown fires, create their own winds, as they draw air in rapidly. Sometimes these winds, although local, can be as fierce as a hurricane. In certain conditions, tornadoes called 'fire whirls' can start within a wildfire, as air roars up in a spiral, carrying flames with it.

Rotating fire column

Cold air sucked in

DANGEROUS SPARKS

Fires can be started in many ways. They can start naturally when lightning from a summer thunderstorm sets vegetation alight, or with hot cinders from a volcanic eruption. But many fires are ignited by people, either carelessly with a dropped match or a camp fire, or deliberately by arsonists to cause mayhem.

EXTREME WILDFIRE DAMAGE

Wildfires can be very dangerous indeed. For people, there is not only the intense heat of the flames, but also the suffocating smoke. Fires destroy houses and almost anything else that gets in their way. And their effect on wildlife – on forest-dwelling creatures and plants – can be more devastating than any other natural disaster.

UNBELIEVABLE!

There is rarely just one fire in a wildfire, because hot material spreads on the wind to start fires in multiple places. The Black Saturday fire that engulfed the bush in Australia in 2009 involved 400 separate fires.

BURNED OUT

Wildfires spread fast and can quickly change direction. People fleeing by car may misjudge which way a fire is spreading, get lost in the smoke or find their route blocked by flames. That's why it is vital to listen to warnings from the authorities and get out of the area early if you're ever close to a wildfire.

REBIRTH

For some plants and animals, a fire is not a disaster but an opportunity. The fire clears away dead wood, and makes room for new plants. Many forests bounce back after a fire. Jackpines, white pines and yellow birch have their seeds opened up and given a nutritious new ash-rich soil.

ANIMAL TRAGEDY

For many forest creatures, a wildfire is a disaster. Birds may fly away. Bigger mammals may run. Some creatures may burrow into the ground, or take cover under rock or in water. But young and small animals face certain death, especially tree-dwelling animals like squirrels.

BIG BURN

In 1910, fire engulfed 3 million acres in Idaho, Montana and Washington and killed at least 85 people. Whole towns were burned away, and hundreds of soldiers were brought in to try and stop the flames. From then on, the Forest Service determined to put out every fire. But now many fire experts think this is not only dangerous for firefighters but does little to save forests.

Avery, Idaho →

FIGHTING AN EXTREME WILDFIRE

Wildfires very quickly get out of control and burn over such a vast area that it is hard to fight them — and very dangerous to do so. Different fires need different approaches, but the basic idea is always the same — to rob the fire of its fuel, so that it eventually burns out by itself.

EYEWITNESS

Firefighter Drew Miller stops fires by burning away their fuel source, and uses "chainsaws... to remove fuel sources and dig lines so the fire can't spread as easily. Then we clear the area behind our friendly fire."

FIRE MAP

Computer and satellite technology have enabled experts to keep an ever closer eye on wildfires in the USA. They can now show live, interactive maps of just where a wildfire is burning at any one time. The high concentration of fires in the forest regions of the north-west becomes very clear this way.

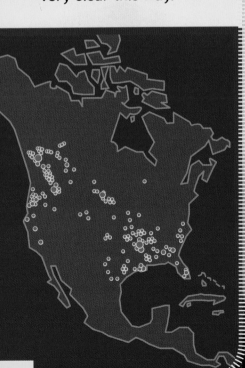

CHOPPER DROP

Special helicopters are sometimes flown over the fire to dump water, fire retardant and other chemicals, such as ammonium phosphate, that slow down fires. They may water bomb fires with as much as 7,000 litres (2,000 US gals) at a time. They are not trying to put out the fire, though — just buying the ground crew time to create a break in the wood to stop the fire.

WATCHING FOR SMOKE

In forest areas prone to wildfires, watchtowers are often built so that fire-watchers can keep an eye on every potential fire. They might track and record a lightning strike, then keep scanning the horizon for plumes of smoke.

EARLY WARNING

Satellite technology means people are much less likely to be caught by surprise than in the past. Sensitive satellites monitor slight changes in the colour tone of the forest that might indicate smoke. They can then feed this into national wildfire monitoring systems to issue people nearby with a warning.

FIREFIGHTERS

Fighting a fire on the ground is a very dangerous job, and requires a high degree of training. Firefighters are given special protective clothing, such as shirts and trousers made of Nomex, and oxygen supplies to help them when they breathe in the smoke.

FIRE DANGER TODAY

LOW — MODERATE — HIGH — EXTREME

EXTREME WILDFIRE STORY

Wildfire disasters can strike out of the blue. On 1 May 2016, the town of Fort McMurray in Alberta, Canada, suddenly found itself facing utter destruction as a wildfire raged in the forests beyond. Miraculously, only two people died, yet 2,400 houses were destroyed and the disaster was the costliest in Canadian history, at $3.58 billion.

EYEWITNESS

Fire Officer Bendfeld: "I was watching a fire that was going across the trees... it was moving at 28 metres per hour. Then it was going at 32 metres per hour, then 300 metres per hour... How do you get a hold of that?"

EYEWITNESS

Text messages between Jody Butz out firefighting and his wife and 15-year-old son Wesley stuck at school, realizing they might lose their home:

Butz: *Lock down the school and stay with the boys. Be strong.*

Wesley: *Is the fire east of the golf course... toward the house?*

(Butz knew it was, but couldn't be sure where it would end up.)

Butz: *It's coming. Be brave.*

FIRE HELL

Fires are likely in dense, dry forest in hot weather. But the wind made the Fort McMurray fire especially frightening and hard for firefighters. High winds scattered hot embers, starting new fires in unexpected places. They also whipped up flames, so a fire eating slowly forwards suddenly flared up and roared through the trees.

GET OUT OF THERE!

At first, the fire seemed to be under control. Then on the afternoon of 3 May, the wind changed direction and the fire, nicknamed 'The Beast', roared back, heading straight for the town. The government ordered every one of Fort McMurray's 80,000 inhabitants to leave at once and placed some of the evacuees in lodge camps.

Fort McMurray

ROADBLOCK

With the fire forever changing direction, the authorities were not sure which way to send people trying to flee the fire. The police set road blocks to stop them heading into even more danger. Vast traffic jams built up at the blocks. Many people stuck there were frightened and angry, sitting on the highway while their homes and livelihoods burned.

FIRE FROM ABOVE!

A satellite view shows the huge plumes of smoke billowing from the Fort McMurray fire. By mid-May the fire had spread into neighbouring Saskatchewan. By late June, rain and cooler weather and the extraordinary work of the firefighters had brought the fire under control. But they guessed it would take till spring 2017 to put it out altogether.

COASTAL FLOODING

Low-lying coasts are very vulnerable to flooding from the sea. Sea water may be pushed on to land by strong winds and hurricanes. And the flooding may be even worse if the winds are carrying heavy rain. Some of the most devastating coastal floods, though, come from tsunamis – vast waves set in motion by earthquakes under the sea.

KATRINA FLOOD

When Hurricane Katrina struck New Orleans in August 2005, it wasn't the winds that did the real damage but the flooding that came a day later. The waterways running through the city were filled to bursting by the combination of the storm surge (see opposite) and the heavy rain brought by the storm. Finally, the levees, the barriers containing the water, burst and the water flooded into the city.

STORM SURGE

Powerful storms, especially hurricanes, can cause a sudden and dramatic rise in the sea, called a storm surge. It's like a super-high tide. Low air pressure in the storm's centre makes the sea swell upwards, and high winds push water towards the shore and build up waves. Storm surges can briefly raise the sea level many metres, swamping coastal areas.

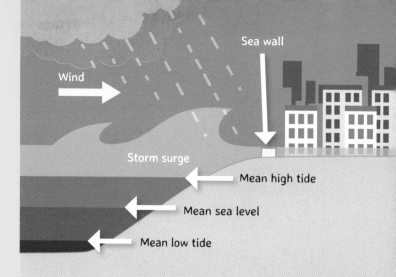

Wind

Sea wall

Storm surge

Mean high tide

Mean sea level

Mean low tide

STORM WAVES

Even without a storm surge, storms can bring monster waves that smash against sea defences and may breach them. But when these waves coincide with a high tide or a storm surge, they can bring devastating floods

HIGH WATER

The height of sea tides varies as the Moon makes its month-long journey round the Earth. They are at their most extreme during 'spring tides' when, twice a month, the Moon is in line with the Sun. Then, the gravitational pull of the Moon and Sun combines to raise and lower the sea dramatically. In between come more moderate 'neap tides', when the Moon and Sun pull at right angles.

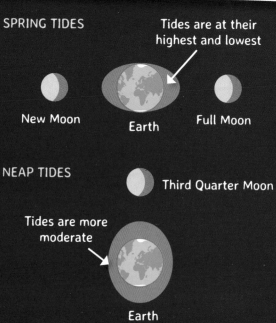

SPRING TIDES

Tides are at their highest and lowest

Sun

New Moon

Earth

Full Moon

NEAP TIDES

Third Quarter Moon

Tides are more moderate

Sun

Earth

First Quarter Moon

RIVER FLOODING

Floods happen when there is too much water to run away safely through drains and rivers. They almost always follow heavy rain or melting snow. Then rivers or lakes may overflow, or there may be too much rain for it to soak into the ground and so it builds up on land.

UNBELIEVABLE!

Some of the most disastrous floods have been dam bursts. In 1979, the Machchu-2 dam in Gujarat, India, suddenly collapsed after heavy rain and the lake behind the dam poured through. A wall of water swept through the nearby town of Morbi, killing 25,000 people.

FLASH FLOODS

Most floods develop slowly, but 'flash floods' occur in just a few hours or even minutes! They start with rain so heavy it cannot soak into the ground fast enough. Instead, it runs straight off in a surge powerful enough to wash away cars, bridges and buildings! Most flash floods occur after sudden storms in dry areas. Sometimes, flash floods occur in damp areas, too, as this diagram shows.

Heavy rain falls on ground that is already waterlogged

High river due to high rainfall

Rainfall cannot soak into the ground and runs straight off into the river

The river quickly rises and bursts its banks

Extra river pressure feeds into low-lying areas through sink holes

SNOWMELT

In spring, winter snow in the mountains melts and fills local rivers with water. If the temperature rises and melts the snow rapidly, it can unleash dramatic floods. In 1997 in North America, a sudden snowmelt made the Red River of the North rise and swamp vast areas of Minnesota, North Dakota and Manitoba, including the cities of Grand Forks and East Grand Forks.

BLOCKED DRAINS

In most cities, drains are designed to carry rain safely away. But sometimes they get blocked, or rain falls so heavily that drains cannot cope. The result is local floods that can ruin homes and businesses. Occasionally, rain is not the culprit. Water supply pipes can burst and create local floods.

WOOD STRIPPING

Some areas have become more prone to flooding in recent years — and one reason is that trees have been extensively cut down. Trees hold rainwater on the land, and give it time to soak safely into the ground. But if they are felled to make way for farmland or to use the timber, there is nothing to hold the water. Instead it runs straight off, swelling rivers and causing flooding.

19

EXTREME FLOOD DAMAGE

Floods can have a devastating effect. Terrible floods in China have claimed many millions of lives. But even when people escape alive, homes and businesses can be wrecked and lives torn apart, and the impact can last for years after the flood waters have receded.

EARLY DAMAGE

Floods have many immediate effects. Some people are drowned or stranded and may have to be rescued by boat or helicopter. Buildings and structures such as bridges and roads are damaged or even washed away. Power lines may be damaged, too, so even areas that are not actually flooded suffer.

WATER SHORTAGE

You might think water is the last thing people need in a flood. But flooding disrupts clean water supplies — and the flood waters are usually too contaminated to drink. Flood waters pick up toxic substances as they flow over the land, and become polluted with sewage.

FLOOD DISEASE

Many deaths from floods are caused not by drowning but by diseases that follow. Germs spread in the polluted water and, with little clean drinking water, people succumb to diseases such as cholera. Malaria (being tested for here) can also spread in the stagnant pools left behind.

DOWN BELOW

The lower levels of buildings — basements and cellars — are often the worst-hit by floods. Because they are below ground level, they are hard to drain. Homes with flooded basements are often ruined because it is so difficult to dry them out. The dampness can cause diseases related to breathing.

BROKEN BRIDGES

Bridges span rivers, so are particularly vulnerable to flooding. Some may simply be swamped. Others may be broken as the power of the surging waters washes away the bridge supports. Bridges are vital lines of communication, and the loss of a bridge can trap people, or prevent supplies getting in.

ONE STEP AHEAD OF THE FLOOD

It is not easy to predict when a flood is going to occur. Forecasting the weather is tricky enough. But forecasting when a storm will bring flooding is even harder. All the same, experts are now monitoring rainfall patterns continually and using satellites to help them spot likely flood spots. At the same time, authorities in flood-prone areas are looking at ways of preventing floods

UNBELIEVABLE!

A 10-year flood is a moderate flood likely to occur every 10 years or so. A huge 100-year flood is likely to occur once every century. But if you're unlucky you could get two '100-year' floods in a few years!

STORM WATCH

Hurricanes often bring flooding if they strike the coast in flat, low-lying areas. By analysing past storms, experts can tell how likely flooding is. By tracking an incoming storm by satellite, and using reports from weather stations and other data, weather forecasters can guess how intense it is and where it is likely to hit land. They can then issue flood warnings.

GLOBAL FLOOD WATCH

The Global Flood Monitoring System, or GFMS, provides a continually updated computer map showing how likely flooding is anywhere in the world. It monitors where rain is falling and how streams are flowing. Satellites also watch where water is building up on land.

THE WEEK'S RAINFALL AROUND THE WORLD
Little or no rain   Most rain

FLOODPLAIN

In lowlands, most rivers wind their way through a 'floodplain'. This is a broad, flat area that stretches away on either side of the river. It was built up over thousands of years by silt dropped as the river overflowed its banks again and again, and flooded the landscape. As their name implies, floodplains are very prone to flooding. But a detailed knowledge of the floodplain can tell experts exactly which areas are likely to flood.

Modelled Flood Depth (M)

	<0.5
	0.5 - 1.0
	1.0 - 2.0
	2.0 - 4.0

Full Extent Of Floor

FLOOD CONTROL

In places liable to flooding, people often put up barriers to stop the water. Dams may be erected across rivers to hold up the flow at flood times and release the water gradually. Rivers may be channelled between high walls and flood barriers. Barriers may also be built on the coast to prevent the sea flooding in. Across the River Thames in London, a huge lifting gate called the Thames Barrier (inset) can be lowered quickly to prevent a storm surge out at sea coming up the river and flooding the city.

EXTREME FLOOD STORY

Bangladesh is a low-lying country that is very vulnerable to flooding. Almost three-quarters of the land is less than 8 m (26 ft) above sea level. Floods have struck Bangladesh again and again, but one of the worst events was in 2004. It lasted from July to September and at its worst covered nearly half the country in water.

FLOODING BANGLADESH

There are many reasons Bangladesh is flooded so often. One is its monsoon climate, which means most of its rain is concentrated in one season of the year. Another is the spring melting of heavy snow in the Himalayan mountains. In 2004, the main cause of flooding was a long period of heavy rain that made all three of its big rivers peak at the same time.

BANGLADESH

Snow melts in the mountains, releasing a lot of water into the river

Monsoon climate brings heavy rains

Much land in the mountains has been cleared of forest, increasing water run-off

Three giant rivers cover 10 per cent of Bangladesh

Soil eroded from areas stripped of forest washes into rivers and chokes them

Urban development has reduced the amount of soft land that can soak up water

Global warming has raised sea levels and increased snowmelt and rainfall

FLOOD RELIEF

This picture shows how used to flooding the people of Bangladesh have become. Women stand patiently in a queue in waist-deep water to collect supplies of food. In 2004, food relief was vital because the floods destroyed millions of tons of rice and drove many people close to starvation.

Although comparatively few people lost their lives in the floods, they caused huge disruption to life. Homes, livestock sheds, haystacks, vegetable gardens and paddy fields were damaged and destroyed. Many people had to wade through the waters with nothing but their clothes and move into makeshift shelters on higher, drier land or into school buildings, or stay with relatives for months or even years.

STRANDED

The waters rose suddenly, with little warning. Many people were trapped and only escaped by climbing on to the roofs of buildings. They waited for days to be rescued, without food or clean drinking water.

INTENSE FUTURES

In recent years, it seems that wildfires and floods have been becoming more and more frequent and extreme. There have always been serious floods and fires in the past, so this might be coincidence. But many experts are convinced that the way we manage the land is at least partly to blame. So, too, is our changing climate. Are there even more devastating fires and floods to come?

UNBELIEVABLE!
Although global warming is priming forests for more wildfires, most of the recent megafires were started by people. Some were accidents, but many were started deliberately to clear land for farming – then got out of hand.

IF THE ICE SHEETS MELTED...

Some experts believe the Earth could warm up so much that the polar ice sheets could melt entirely. If so, all the water would raise sea levels dramatically. If the Arctic ice sheet melted, sea levels would rise 6 m (20 ft) or so worldwide. If the Antarctic ice sheet melted too, sea levels would rise 60 m (200 ft)! That would drown the USA's east coast, including New York and Florida.

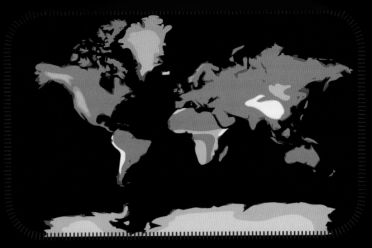

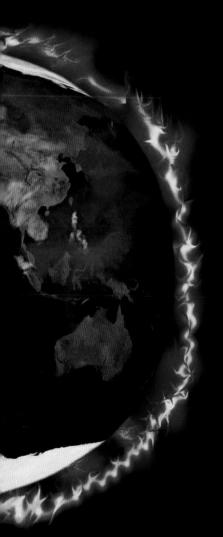

THE AGE OF THE MEGAFIRES

Across the world, devastating wildfires seem to be breaking out more and more often — and they are getting bigger and bigger, too. Experts think the steady warming of the world's climate is to blame for these 'megafires'. The warmer climate makes for longer, drier summers, more fuel for fires as plants grow and dry out, and more lightning as thunderstorms occur more frequently. And, of course, hotter weather primes forests for a conflagration.

LOSING THE MALDIVES

Over the last few decades, as the world has got warmer, the sea has been rising as glaciers and ice sheets melt, and the water in the oceans expands. Experts believe that sea levels are rising by almost 1 cm (0.4 in) every year in the Indian Ocean. That doesn't sound much, but it would be enough to drown the beautiful Maldive Islands within the next century, as they are on average just 1 m (3 ft) above sea level.

TIMELINE

1910
The Big Burn raged across 12,000 km² (4,700 square miles) in Idaho and Montana, USA, killing 87 people

1287
St Lucia's flood was a huge storm tide that swamped northern Holland and Germany and claimed 80,000 lives

1887
The Yellow River (Huang He) in China flooded in the second deadliest flood of all time, claiming up to 2 million lives

1911
The Yangtze river in China flooded, taking 100,000 lives

1918
The Cloquet Fire in Minnesota, USA, devastated farmland, railway yards and towns, killing 551 people

1864
The Great Sheffield Flood claimed the lives of over 240 people in Sheffield, England, in minutes, as the Dale Dyke Dam failed

1931
The Yangtze river in China flooded again in the deadliest natural disaster of all time, killing up to 4 million people

1287 •

1871
The Great Peshtigo Fire, the worst in US history, raged through Wisconsin and Michigan, USA

1530
St Felix's flood swamped much of the Netherlands and Belgium and claimed over 100,000 lives

The Great Dayton Flood devastated Dayton, Ohio

1362
St Marcellus's flood was a storm tide that covered vast areas of the Netherlands and created an inland sea, the Zuiderzee

1889
In the Johnstown flood, over 2,000 people lost their lives when the South Fork Dam collapsed after heavy rain and flooded Johnstown, Pennsylvania

1938
The Yellow River (Huang He) in China flooded again in the third deadliest flood ever, killing 800,000 people

1939
The Black Friday bushfire devastated huge areas of Victoria in Australia

2015
The December floods in Missouri and the Midwest, USA, caused over $3 billion in damage

1975
The Banqiao Dam in China collapsed after Typhoon Nina, unleashing a wave of water that ultimately claimed the lives of nearly 250,000 people

2009
The Black Saturday bushfire devastated 4,400 km² (1,700 square miles) of Victoria in Australia, killing 173 people

2016
Flooding devastated Louisiana, USA, in one of the worst natural disasters of recent years

● **2017**

1971
The Hanoi and Red River Delta flood in Vietnam killed over 100,000 people

1997
The Operation Haze fires in Indonesia were the worst in modern times

2003
Hundreds of fires broke out across Siberia, creating the biggest fire ever known

2016
The town of Fort McMurray in Alberta, Canada, was lucky to escape with only partial damage after a devastating wildfire

2011
The floods from Hurricane Irene caused huge damage to the USA's Atlantic coast

FIERY AND WET

Amazing facts about fires and floods

HOT LOVE

Fire beetles have their very own heat detectors that use infrared to find burning forest fires. But instead of running away, they head for the fire! Once they're in the thick of it, the beetles mate and lay eggs in the scorched trees. The dead trees are good homes for the beetles, because the sap that usually stops them burrowing has been boiled.

GASSED

One of the big problems for firefighters tackling a big blaze is not the heat but the gases released. The biggest danger is carbon monoxide, which is colourless and odourless and therefore hard to detect. Breathing in carbon monoxide can cause headaches, dizziness, nausea and decreased mental functioning, and may even be fatal.

FIRE STARTERS

Wildfires can often start naturally, by lightning or by hot lava. But the US National Park Service fire department believes that up to 90 per cent of wildfires are caused by humans. People may leave campfires unattended, throw away glowing cigarettes or carelessly burn rubbish. Some fires are even started deliberately.

GOOD FLOODS

In many parts of the world, the natural flooding of river plains and deltas each year is a vital part of a farmer's life. The waters bring nutrient-rich silt deposits that create very fertile alluvial soils. In ancient times, many farming communities relied heavily on the annual flooding of floodplain valleys on rivers such as the Nile, Tigris-Euphrates and Ganges.

FLASH POWER

The power of moving water in flash floods can be very dangerous. Water moving at just 16 km/h (10 mph) can exert the same pressure as a gust of wind at tornado speed: 434 km/h (270 mph). The water in flash floods can easily move rocks of 45 kg (100 lb) or more. They can hurl these and other objects at structures with tremendous force – and at people unlucky enough to be caught in the water.

RISING FLOODS

Floods are becoming super-costly in the USA. Between 2011 and 2015, the country was hit by 10 major floods, including Hurricane Irene. They caused $34 billion worth of damage.

WORST WILDFIRES

DEADLIEST IN US HISTORY
The Great Peshtigo Fire, Wisconsin/Michigan, USA
October 1871
Cost in lives: at least 1,500
Area: over 15,300 km² (5,900 square miles)

DEADLIEST IN MODERN TIMES
Operation Haze, Indonesia
1997
Cost in lives: 241 people
Area: over 800,300 km² (31,000 square miles)

DEADLIEST THIS CENTURY
The Black Saturday bushfire,
Victoria, Australia
7 February 2009
Cost in lives: 173
Area: over 4,400 km² (1,700 square miles)

MOST EXPENSIVE THIS CENTURY
Fort McMurray, Alberta, Canada
May 2016
Financial cost: $3.58 billion

WORST FLOODS

DEADLIEST EVER
Yangtze River Flood,
Yangtze River, China
1931
Cost in lives: up to 4 million – the deadliest ever natural disaster

SECOND DEADLIEST
Yellow River Flood, Huang He
River, China
September 1887
Cost in lives: 900,000 to 2 million

DEADLIEST HISTORIC FLOOD
St. Felix's Flood, Flanders and
Zeeland, Netherlands
5 November 1530
Cost in lives: more than 100,000

DEADLIEST IN RECENT YEARS
Banqiao Dam, Henan, China
August 1975
Cost in lives: up to 250,000

INDEX

THE AUTHOR

John Farndon is Royal Literary Fellow at City&Guilds in London, UK, and the author of a huge number of books for adults and children on science, technology and nature, including such international best-sellers as *Do Not Open* and *Do You Think You're Clever?* He has been shortlisted six times for the Royal Society's Young People's Book Prize for a science book, with titles such as *How the Earth Works, What Happens When?* and *Project Body* (2016)